People at Work

Working in the Army

Andrew Langley

Photography by
Chris Fairclough

Wayland

First published in 1982 by
Wayland Publishers Limited,
49 Lansdowne Place, Hove,
East Sussex BN3 1HF, England

© Copyright 1982 Wayland Publishers Limited

ISBN 0 85340 982 X

Phototypeset by Kalligraphics Limited,
Redhill, Surrey
Printed and bound in Great Britain by
R.J.Acford, Chichester

Contents

The British Army today

The British Army has active units in Northern Ireland, Hong Kong, Belize and Gibraltar as well as those of B.A.O.R. in West Germany.

The British Army today has the same job to do that it has always had – protecting its country against attack. But in the modern world this is a lot more complicated than it seems. To protect our own shores, a large part of the Army is stationed in West Germany, joined with other forces of the North Atlantic Treaty Organization to meet the threat from the Communist countries of Eastern Europe. Other units are in Northern Ireland, helping to control terrorist violence there. There are British Army bases in several small countries throughout the world, such as Hong Kong, Belize, Cyprus and Gibraltar.

To do this job effectively, the Army has had to become more skilful and efficient than ever before. It is, in all senses of the word, a professional Army, made up entirely of volunteers who are hand-picked after a number of tests and interviews.

During the Second World War, hundreds of thousands of civilians were 'called up' to serve in the Army, Navy and Air Force. Conscription, as it was called, went on for a long time afterwards as well, and only ended in 1960. Up to that time, every man was required by law to do two years' National Service in one of the armed forces when he reached the age of eighteen and a half.

This meant that the size of the Army was maintained. But it also meant that huge numbers of soldiers were doing something they didn't want to do, and many of them were unsuited to military life anyway. So in order to turn them into soldiers there was a lot of harsh and sometimes petty discipline – hours of 'square-bashing', spud-peeling and being yelled at by purple-faced sergeant majors.

Nowadays, every soldier has chosen to join the Army of his or her own free will, and has been trained into a highly-skilled member of a team. A soldier's time is too valuable to waste on routine chores. It is far more important that he should be learning about the latest self-loading rifle or field radio, rather than peeling potatoes (there are machines to do that now).

In fact, it is becoming increasingly hard to get into the Army, because the use of modern weapons and other equipment demands a high degree of ability from a recruit. Once accepted, the new soldier can sign on for three, six or nine years and, if he wants, stay on for a full term of twenty-two years. He is free to give a year's notice if he wants to leave.

Every recruit, whether a cook or an infantryman, starts off by being given a basic military training, to turn him into a raw fighting soldier. After that, he goes on to learn his trade, which will either be as a combat soldier, or as one of the many specialist tradesmen who play a vital role in supporting and supplying the fighting troops.

In this book, you will meet twelve people who have learned their trades in the Army. For many jobs, this is the best training available, and most soldiers will be able to go straight into a skilled civilian job when they leave the service. The qualifications gained in certain Army trades are recognized by industry and trade unions.

The band of the Royal Scots Guards rehearses for the Trooping the Colour ceremony at their barracks in Victoria, London.

The British Army of the Rhine

The Royal Green Jackets on an exercise in West Germany.

The United Kingdom is part of the North Atlantic Treaty Organization (NATO), which is aimed at providing a military answer to the forces of the Warsaw Pact countries, including the Soviet Union and East Germany. The threat posed by the 'Iron Curtain' countries is a very big one. In East Germany, there are 20 combat-ready Soviet Army divisions and 6 East German divisions; in Czechoslovakia, there are 15 divisions, and in Poland 17 divisions.

Altogether, there are 950,000 soldiers of the Warsaw Pact countries stationed in central Europe. They also have 17,500 tanks and 2,700 tactical aircraft, many more than the NATO forces, and these numbers are being increased all the time.

To counterbalance this huge army, the NATO countries have large numbers of their own troops and weapons permanently stationed in West Germany. One of the most important parts of this is the British Army of the Rhine (B.A.O.R.), with a strength of 55,000 men.

In peacetime, B.A.O.R. is divided into three parts. The first, and largest, is the 1st (British) Corps, which is the fighting element of the Army. It is made up of five divisions, and is equipped with over 600 Chieftain tanks and nearly 3,000 other armoured vehicles. Each division contains a reconnaissance regiment, which uses fast armoured vehicles called Scorpion and Scimitar, two armoured regiments of Chieftain tanks, infantry battalions, who travel in armoured personnel carriers, and an artillery group, who use everything from field howitzers to anti-tank missiles. A regiment of Royal Engineers is also included, and their job is to lay minefields and create obstacles for the enemy.

The second main part of B.A.O.R. is stationed in the British sector of Berlin. There are about 3,000 soldiers there who, together with French and United States troops, look after Western interests in the city.

The third section is called Rhine Area, and it is the soldiers who work in the Rhine Area that this book is mainly about. The district covers the Rhineland and the Rühr and has its headquarters at Düsseldorf. Within it are some 125 units who do not actually fight, but who are vital in keeping the fighting troops going by providing them with stores, main-

taining their equipment and looking after their transport.

Also in the Rhine Area is the headquarters for the whole of the B.A.O.R. This is a huge camp at Rheindahlen, near Düsseldorf, which has a population of some 13,000, including families. The Royal Air Force and the Northern Army Group also have their H.Q. here.

Most British soldiers enjoy the chance of a spell living in Germany. Married men will almost always have their wives and families with them, and Germany is an ideal centre for seeing the rest of Europe – places like Switzerland, Holland, and France are all within easy reach. Relations with the German people are very good, and in fact there are 1,800 British soldiers who have married German women.

There is always plenty of sport going on in the Army. This is a six-a-side tournament being held at Rheindahlen in West Germany.

9

'Nobby' Clarke
Military policeman

Melvyn 'Nobby' Clarke is 26. He is a corporal in the Military Police and is stationed in Düsseldorf, where he helps keep law and order amongst the huge numbers of military personnel in the area.

I was born in a village near Doncaster in South Yorkshire. When I left school at 15, I had no 'O' levels or anything. Around there, if all else fails, it's down the pit you go, as it is a famous mining area. But there was never any danger of that with me. Like most small boys I liked playing soldiers – I reckon I've never really finished with that! However, I didn't want to go straight into the Army as a boy soldier: I thought I would wait until I was 17 and go into what is called man service.

When I left school I started off as a trainee manager for Woolworth's, and then went on to be a storeman for a builders' suppliers. They were both pretty humdrum jobs, though, and the idea of life in the Army seemed a much more exciting one. There was no pressure from my family – in fact my father was never in the Army during the war because he was a farmer, which was a reserved occupation.

I did my training at the Royal Military Police depot at Chichester in Sussex. First of all, there was the basic military training, which teaches you discipline, how to take the pimples out of your boots with a hot spoon and all that, and turns you out as a trained soldier.

The next phase was learning police work. This is very much the same as civilian police training, except for two important things. A military policeman (M.P.) carries a pistol with him, and he has to learn how to deal with Army officers who may be senior to him in rank. We spend a lot of time firing on the ranges, and being taught how to maintain our weapons, which always have to be cleaned after firing. We have very strict orders about opening fire with them, and only rarely do we have to. I've never fired mine throughout my career – except on the ranges.

As for dealing with officers, that can be difficult. We have power over any offender, even someone senior in rank to us, and here the key word is politeness, as it is with the civilian police. If you're polite and pay respect where it's due, from the private right up to the most senior officer, you should never have any problems. That's what I was always taught.

In police training, the arrest is the basic act. And every time you make an arrest, you've got to use the minimum of force necessary to make it effective. If no force is necessary, you don't use any force. I find that if you approach people in the right manner, you will usually get the right response from them. Of course, you do get the odd occasion where force is needed. I was taught various police holds, and was trained in aikido – an ancient Japanese form of self defence. But it is important that no unnecessary injury is caused.

From the depot at Chichester I passed out as a lance corporal in the Military Police. Every new policeman is automatically promoted to lance corporal – it gives them a little bit of authority to start them off. Roughly eighteen months later, when they've gained a bit of experience, they're promoted to corporal, provided they're up to the standard required.

The first posting is always a big step for any soldier. Mine was to Detmold, north of where I am now. I was only 18 years old, and very nervous to start with. In the depot, I was taught everything by the book, but of course I'd no experience at all of actually dealing with people. I was thrown right in at the deep end.

The M.P. lance corporal has the power of arrest in his warrant card. At first, like me, they can seem very nosey and starchy, but all they are doing is putting into practice what they've learned. The commonsense part of it only comes later, when you can relax and be more natural with people. But until then you have to go by the book, and that can often

Nobby talks with one of his colleagues on a patrol bike.

Nobby on the beat at an Army camp in Düsseldorf.

One in every four M.P.s in Düsseldorf is a woman.

M.P.s on exercise wearing their special nuclear, biological and chemical (N.B.C.) suits.

annoy other trained soldiers.

After my spell in Detmold, I was posted to Northern Ireland for two years, and then to Cyprus for two years. Now I'm back in Germany again as a full corporal, and enjoying my work a lot. Obviously I would like to be promoted up to sergeant, which could happen in the next five years. A sergeant has a lot of desk work to do and is more of an organizer, so he has much less chance of getting out on the beat. Not everybody wants this sort of work and some M.P.s spend their whole twenty-two-year term without getting higher than corporal, and no-one thinks badly of them.

I've recently been given command of a section of five men. Sometimes, of course, we get WRAC policewomen, and in fact one in every four M.P.s here is a woman. I've got one in my section just now, and I can tell you that they're every bit as efficient as the men, and every bit as keen, too.

We work on a shift system which might seem rather strange to a civilian. Each cycle lasts for eight days. For the first two days we carry on with our training, doing things like shooting on the ranges, looking after our equipment, and practising what we should do if a real war broke out. In wartime, our role is very different from peacetime. Instead of keeping law and order among military personnel, we would be responsible for helping the Army to move to and from the battle zones, directing traffic and making sure that the roads were open.

Another very important wartime job that we practise is the measuring of damage and contamination after, say, a nuclear attack. On top of our full combat uniform, we wear what is called an N.B.C. (nuclear, biological and chemical warfare) suit. It is made from special cotton, impregnated with charcoal and other chemicals which protect us from nuclear fallout. On our heads we wear a respirator that we breathe through, which will last for twenty-four hours. As you can imagine, it all gets very hot and stuffy at times!

The next two days of our shift is spent on day duty, and these are followed by two nights on patrol. After that, we get two days off to catch up on our sleep and rest, before the cycle starts all over again. Like I said, it may seem strange, but you soon get used to it.

When I'm on duty, the first thing I do is report to the duty sergeant in the office by the main gate of the garrison. The front desk in the M.P. station is the most important place there – that's where all the complaints, queries and reports of crimes come in, and are noted down in the daily occurrences book. Behind the desk is the duty office, where I will be briefed on things that need investigating – stolen vehicles to look out for, soldiers gone AWOL (Absent Without Official Leave), missing children and so on.

We go out on patrol in police cars, usually Ford Cortinas, and there are some motor cycles too, although I don't often get to ride one. We tend to stick to the areas of the city where soldiers usually go. There's one part of Düsseldorf called the *Altstadt*, or Old Town, which is almost completely made up of bars and clubs, so you can always guarantee that we'll keep a close watch there! We get on very well with the German police, and do our best not to tread on their toes.

Over here, one of the most frequent crimes is drunken driving, although there are less cases now than a few years ago. The German police are always very strict on this, and go round looking for drunken drivers. But as far as the Military Police are concerned, looking for them is not the done thing, and we only stop people when we have grounds to suspect them.

There are the other usual crimes, such as

When he reports for duty, Nobby is briefed by the sergeant on his day's work.

The front desk at an M.P. station.

violence and assaults. When we get a complaint or a report, we have to decide whether it is serious enough to tell the Special Investigation Branch about. This is the detective side of our force, which some people see as being more glamorous than being on the beat. If your talents are inclined that way, you could apply to join the S.I.B. after a few years, but I don't think I shall.

The process of arresting and charging someone is much the same as in the civilian police. The main difference is that we don't lock them up here, but take them back to their own barracks, where they can be dealt with. Before that, we will interview them and make notes, and then get them to sign a statement. Later, we make out a report on the crime, which is double-checked and typed up, and then sent to the particular officer in charge of the offender. We don't generally have much to do with the actual court martial, and aren't

British M.P.s work very closely with the German police, but do their best not to get in their way.

often called on to give evidence.

For major incidents, like a riot, we have a mobile control point. This is really a truck with a cabin fixed on the back, which is driven to the scene of the crime. It is set up like a small office, with maps, radio and telephone, and makes it much easier to take statements and give reports on the spot.

We have two other weapons apart from the pistol which we are trained to use for situations such as a riot. One is the good old truncheon. We have to be very careful with these, because any mark or scratch on them has to be recorded and accounted for – you can't just go around bashing people. The other is the very accurate self-loading rifle, which would only be used as a last resort.

Riots are not often aimed directly at the Military Police, but we are usually in the middle of them, trying to keep order. And that just about sums up this job. You're nobody's friend basically – the lads come to expect it, and shrug it off as a joke, most likely. After all, that's what they call a policeman's lot.

Tom Clare
Movement controller

Tom Clare is 38 and a staff sergeant in the Royal Corps of Transport currently stationed in Düsseldorf. He is responsible for organizing the movement of troops and vehicles throughout the military area.

For someone whose job is moving people about, I've done a fair bit of moving about myself. I've been in the Army for nineteen years now, and in that time I've worked in forty-eight different countries. The day after I got married, for example, I was flown out to Rhodesia (now Zimbabwe) to help monitor the ceasefire after the civil war they had there a few years ago. I was then back in England for two weeks, when I moved house, before being sent to Kenya. After that, I had a break of four weeks before being sent out to Canada.

Travel is one of the big perks of this job, of course. But it wasn't the main reason why I joined the Army in the first place. When I left school at 16, I had six 'O' levels, and I wanted to become a professional footballer. Preston North End took me on as an apprentice, though I never got higher than the third team, and after three years I was simply told that I wouldn't make it in football.

The Army was more or less the next thing that came to mind, and the Royal Engineers (R.E.) seemed the best place to learn a trade. My brother and my cousins were also in the Army, and that helped me to make my decision. As they were all in infantry regiments, I thought I would be different and go into the Engineers.

Everyone who joins the Army has to go through a series of tests, which find out things like your I.Q., your physical fitness, and how practical you are. The personnel selection officer then looks at your results and tries to fit you into the particular trade that suits you best. In my case, this was office work, and I was guided towards the job of clerk.

Before I got down to that, of course, I had to do my basic military training. This lasted for six weeks, and consisted of all the things that every recruit has to learn, like drilling and handling weapons, plus the special R.E. training. Every Royal Engineer has to qualify

Tom greets soldiers and their families as they arrive at the airport in Düsseldorf.

He sees them on to a bus that will take them to the camp where they are stationed.

as what they call a combat engineer, and is taught all about constructing roads, laying mines and building bridges. This was all completely new to me, and I learned an awful lot.

Then I went on to my trade training at the Royal Engineers depot at Longmoor in Hampshire. As a clerk I was taught typing and other office skills, and also about movement control. This is simply the moving of men and machines about the world by sea, air, road or rail in the most efficient possible manner. There's plenty of paperwork involved, and you have to be a methodical sort of person to be good at it.

My first posting was two years in the south of England, working on troop movements at the London airports. Then, in 1965, I went abroad for the first time, to work in the port at Malta. At the same time, I was promoted to lance corporal and was transferred, with the whole of the movement control organization, from the Engineers to the newly-formed Royal Corps of Transport. Next, I went to Libya for two years, and worked with the aircraft and shipping at Benghazi: we had to leave there early because of the Arab-Israeli war.

I did even more travelling in my next job, which was with a mobile movements unit. For four years I was constantly on the move, and worked in a lot of different countries. On top of all that, my next posting was to Hong Kong! There I was made up to full sergeant, and did a lot of work at the harbour. In 1978 I joined another mobile unit, where I was sent on one of the best jobs I've ever had – four months in Zimbabwe before the independence celebrations. That's one place I would like to go back to.

Finally, in 1981, I was posted out here to Germany – the first time I've been with B.A.O.R. in nineteen years of service. This is more or less my last tour of duty, because my twenty-two-year term is up in 1985, so I won't be sent anywhere else abroad now.

In the two years I've been here I've done every job in this place, which is the trooping centre for the whole Rhine Area. The job I'm doing now is N.C.O. in charge of surface movement in the area – that means travel by sea, road or rail. In the office next door they deal with movement by air. We usually alternate between the jobs every six to nine months so that we don't become stale.

My main work is the organizing of the day-to-day movement of men and units stationed in B.A.O.R. Troops are always moving around, on exercises, or to different training areas. When a convoy is planned, we have to get special licences for them to move on the German roads. Luckily enough, I've got a civilian assistant who deals with the German police and Army to get the necessary authority. He's an Englishman who has lived in Germany ever since the War, and is on very good terms with them. Even so, it takes ten working days for the licences to come through, so everything has to be plotted for weeks ahead. If it is something extremely urgent, you can do it by signal or by telephone.

Planning is vital in all this. For example, a programme of training for the Territorial Army is sent to us every year by our H.Q. in Britain. This tells us well in advance which units are coming out to Germany to do some training. Then, about six to eight weeks before they're due to arrive, we get what is called a movement instruction, which gives the dates, times and methods by which they will travel out. Our job is to meet them, and return them to the U.K. when their training is over.

If they are coming by sea, they will be ferried to a port such as Zeebrugge or Rotterdam, and given a route to follow to the German border. We will send a team from here to meet the convoys at the border,

Tom checks the labels on the baggage of the arriving soldiers.

organize all their paperwork, take them past the customs post, and get them across into Germany.

As you can imagine, there's a mountain of paper needed for all this. Every vehicle has to have something called a 'triptych', which allows them to travel in three countries – Germany, Belgium and Holland. There is a form listing all the stores being carried, which has to be stamped by the customs officials at the borders. And every individual person must have their identity card, and a NATO travel order, which permits them to move through NATO countries.

About a week before the unit is ready to return, we will send them another movement instruction, with details of times, border crossings and ferries. The only time I get out

Tom and a sergeant carefully work out the route for a convoy.

Tom reads out instructions to incoming troops over the public address system.

of the office now is to go and help convoys cross over the border. It makes a nice change from going through the mail and answering queries on the telephone, which is what I spend most of my days doing.

Next door in the air section, things are dealt with in much the same way. We meet people arriving at one of the airports, here at Düsseldorf, or at Brugen, and make sure that there is transport ready to take them to their exercise area. During the summer months there are an awful lot of aircraft coming in and out, and you normally find yourself working at weekends as well. Our hours are flexible, you see, there's no five-day week in the Army. Sometimes you can get really clobbered, and be stuck at an airfield from six in the morning until midnight.

Altogether, we must move somewhere in the region of 25,000 men every year. As well as the normal troop movements, there are special cases, like the meeting of V.I.P.s. When someone very important (such as the General Officer Commanding) arrives at the airport, I take him into the arrivals lounge and make sure that his luggage is taken out to his car.

The other special cases are people going on compassionate leave. If, say, somebody's mother dies, the Army tries to get them home as soon as possible. A bloke can be taken straight from an exercise, put on to an aircraft, met by a car at the other end, and be back home within four hours. It's a marvellous service which I've used myself. I was woken up with bad news in Hong Kong at two o'clock in the morning and put on the first flight back to Britain.

I'll come out of the Army when my twenty-two-year term is up in three years' time. But I've had a good run, and seen far more of the world than the run-of-the-mill soldier. What's more, I shall only be just over forty years old, and will be able to think about a new career with the security of a full Army pension of about £50 a week to rely on.

When I signed on, I was earning less than £3 a week. Now I'm glad to say the pay's much better, and the Army helps you to get into a new line of work by paying for a resettlement course on whatever you want to do. My wife and I have decided we want to run a pub in my home town of Manchester, and I shall be spending my last six months of Army time on a hotel and catering course in Plymouth. It'll be nice to get back to English beer!

A soldier is being hurriedly flown home on compassionate leave. Tom is there to make sure he gets his ticket.

Brian Hearn
Railwayman

Brian Hearn is 42 years old and a squadron quartermaster sergeant with the Royal Corps of Transport. His main job is to train young railwaymen at the depot near Düsseldorf.

In my day, most small boys grew up wanting to be engine drivers. I was brought up in Leeds, and the sight of those great steam locomotives on the Midland Region was an enormous thrill. I left the local secondary school with nothing in the way of 'O' levels or C.S.E.s, and applied straightaway to join British Railways.

I couldn't get in at first, so I got a job at an engineering works. I found this rather boring, and didn't like the prospect of working on a factory floor for the rest of my life. Again I tried B.R., and again I was turned down. This time I went in to the building trade as an apprentice bricklayer, which was all right, but was only as good as the weather.

Eventually I applied a third time to B.R., and at last got in as a cleaner. This really meant that I was an apprentice fireman, but my first job was to clean out the locomotives. I had to get the ash and clinker out, clear the pipes and generally get the engine ready for service. The thrill, as a 15 year old, of working with these giant locomotives and travelling on the footplate was something that no youngerster could realize nowadays. After that, I got to be a fireman, and worked on the Midland Region, firing all sorts of trains, including the famous *Royal Scot*.

I've got to say that joining the Army was something I did on the spur of the moment. Two or three of my railway mates decided to give the Army a crack, and I followed them. One day, I just walked into a recruiting office in Leeds and signed on to join the transportation department of the Royal Engineers. At that time, the system of national service was coming to an end, and they were keen to sign up full-time soldiers.

I did my basic training and my Royal Engineers (R.E.) training at the depot in Hampshire. Being a railwayman I was automatically steered towards the railway side of things. In those days, the railways were much bigger concerns within the Army than they are now. When I joined in 1958 there were three railway regiments, and other operations abroad – especially in the Far East.

My trade training took just under twelve months. Because there was so much railway work then, there were eight different trades, including signalman, traffic operator, steam driver and diesel driver. I chose to go on the footplate again, and as an alternative trade learned about port operating. If I had come into military railways today, I would have done just one course which included all the railway trades.

After a spell as fireman on the Longmoor Military Railway in Hampshire, I was posted to a reserve unit. That was an interesting job, because you were sent wherever you were needed – one day you could be out laying track, another you could be doing a bit of bridge-building. But then the Army railways began to be run down, at the same time that the government was closing so many B.R. branch lines. Worst of all, the steam locomotives were phased out. At the same time, my department was transferred into the new Royal Corps of Transport.

I returned to Longmoor and stayed there for quite a few years. Then I started on the training side of things. I didn't relish this at the time – I was just steered that way – but I wanted to get on, so I set about getting myself qualified for promotion. As I had only had a run-of-the-mill education before I joined up, I decided to do evening classes in various subjects, including English, maths and current affairs. With these, I gained the Certificate of Second Class Education, and began on the promotion ladder.

I was made a full corporal in 1962, and after a spell in Malta I was promoted to sergeant. Then I came out here to Germany for the first

Brian instructs some trainees on the mechanics of one of the squadron's diesel shunters.

Then Brian explains the braking system on a flatwagon.

Brian lends a sympathetic ear to a soldier with a problem.

As squadron quartermaster sergeant, Brian has a lot of administrative work to do.

time, and joined this squadron as a junior instructor. All the time I was pushing myself to get on – once I knew that the Army life was what I wanted, then I set myself a target: to become a sergeant-major. In 1974 I was put up to staff sergeant and sent back to the U.K. depot for further training, where I did an instructors' course and a squadron quartermaster sergeant's course.

Once you get up to the S.Q.M.S. level, and become a warrant officer, you have much more to do with man-management and paperwork. I was trained to organize things like firing on the ranges, to look after the soldiers' welfare and discipline, and to keep all the record books up to date. On top of all that, you've got to learn to accept responsibility. A lot of sergeant-majors have a little notice on their desk saying 'The buck stops here', and that means that all the problems flying around usually end up in their laps, because they know more about the administration of the place than anyone else.

When a vacancy arose out here for an S.Q.M.S. to take over the training, I jumped at the chance. This is now the only railway squadron left within the whole British Army. There are railways in the U.K. which are under the control of the Army Department Rail Services, but they are all actually run by civilians.

In this depot we run two diesel shunters, and have a fleet of 140 flatwagons. The different military departments make bids for the use of these wagons, usually to move heavy equipment around the country. They are loaded by either lifting or driving the piece of equipment on from the stone ramps. Where there is no permanent ramp, we can use a special ramp wagon for the loading. The train is put together by the shunters, and then moved on to a connection with the German railway system, which takes it to its destination where another Army railway crew picks it up.

My job, as I have already said, is mainly to do with training and administration. My day generally starts at eight o'clock, when we have a working parade. I check absentees, and have a look at the blokes' dress. I don't go for the short-back-and-sides haircut – the days of the screaming and shouting sergeant-major are gone – but I like to think that the lads are relatively tidy.

My next priority is a cup of coffee, and then once or twice a week we have what we call an 'orderly room'. This is when the officer commanding (O.C.) interviews soldiers who have offended against the regulations and punishes them if necessary. If a chap is stopped in his car by the M.P.s, for example, and is found to have no licence, we receive a report about it. My job is to frame the charge, so I wade through the book and select the appropriate charge, and then fill out the correct form. If I'm not quite sure about a charge, I can always go for advice to the Army Legal Services.

On the morning of the orderly room, the soldier is taken into the O.C.'s office under escort with all the witnesses. His case is tried by the O.C., and if he is found guilty he is given a suitable punishment. Usually they are minor offences, like disobeying unit orders, or not being in the right place, but if there is any damage done, the offender is told to meet part of the bill out of his own pay – depending on how much he earns.

After all that, I do the mail, and spend the rest of the day working on my training courses. If there are none on at the time, I have to plan the dates and programmes for forthcoming ones. If there are courses going on, I may be down to do several lectures during the day, which could take seven or eight hours to get through. If a course has just

The training centre has its own model railway for trainees.

Brian instructs some WRAC trainees on the securing of loads to flatwagons.

23

Brian with a group of German civilians who work with him at the depot.

finished, I will probably have a lot of marking to do. No two days are the same.

The training year runs from 1st April to 31st March. During that time, we are not only running many courses – at least five in a year – but also continuing to train the blokes here. Every soldier, from the senior officer down to the newest private has to take a series of tests as well to prove his battle fitness. These include firing of weapons, first aid, physical fitness and N.B.C. (nuclear, biological and chemical warfare) training.

I was due to finish my twenty-two-year stint in the Army in 1980, so I applied for a long service appointment to go recruiting back in the U.K. However, I was lucky enough to be asked to continue in regular service. Eventually, I hope to stay on the long service list until the maximum age of fifty-five, which would give me a full Army career with a reasonable pension.

After that, I would like to do something in civvy street to do with people – either a probation officer, or something to do with child welfare. I think I've got a lot of experience of

man-management, but it will be difficult to find a job that will give me as much satisfaction as this one. It's surprising how much satisfaction you get from seeing a 17-year-old lad pass through here for his training, and then maybe come back with a stripe on his arm.

I've got a son of 16, and he goes into the Army this autumn. You can say what you like about the Army, but it's got job security, which is what people are looking for these days. The Army is much more selective now with their recruits, and is paying them a reasonable salary.

I like to spend a lot of my spare time gardening. When I knew I was going to be posted here, I wrote to the married quarters people and asked for a big garden. Nowadays I concentrate on roses – I've got about forty rose bushes – though I do make room for some vegetables. In my younger days I played cricket, football and rugby, and did a lot of swimming. Nowadays, I still run about twenty-five miles a week to keep fit. After that I have a couple of hours in the camp sauna, go home and have my dinner and, in the summer, I can get an hour or two in the garden.

Brian shows two trainees the controls inside the cab of a shunting engine.

David Bashford

Aircraft technician

David Bashford is 36 and has been in the Army for fifteen years. He is now artificer quartermaster sergeant with the Royal Electrical and Mechanical Engineers at Wildenrath airport near Düsseldorf.

There are an awful lot of letters I could put before and after my name. My full title is Warrant Officer Two (A.Q.M.S.) Bashford, R.E.M.E., T.Eng. (C.E.I.), A.F.S.L.A.E.T. All of which goes to show what a lot of technical training I've done in my time, and how many exams I've had to take! I've been in the Army for fifteen years now, and I reckon I must have spent five of those years on courses of one kind or another – not to mention the five-year apprenticeship I went through before I even thought of joining up.

I'm a Londoner (but not quite a cockney) and went to comprehensive school in Dulwich. I left there with no certificates and no idea of what I wanted to do. My father was in the Navy, and I fancied that for a while, but didn't go any further.

I joined a local firm as an apprentice instrument technician, learning to make scientific instruments. I've always had a technical bent, and, when I was a little boy, I was always tinkering away with a spanner, stripping down scooters and so on, trying to find out how things worked. My apprenticeship lasted for five years, at the end of which I gained my City and Guilds qualifications as an instrument technician.

After all that, plus day-release study and evening classes two nights a week, the firm offered me a ridiculous wage, and I thought seriously about the Services. The main reason for this was that I fancied the travelling. I always had an urge to find out what it was like in the Far East. The Army seemed to offer the right balance of trade training, sport, social life and the travelling I wanted.

I joined up with the Royal Electrical and Mechanical Engineers (R.E.M.E.) at the age of twenty-one. After I took an aptitude test to see what I was suited for, they offered me a training in avionics. This is the electronics side of aircraft technology, which I didn't particularly want. I preferred the mechanical side, so I chose to be an aircraft technician on airframes and engines.

After my military training, I went to the School of Electrical and Mechanical Engineering at Bordon in Hampshire for nine months, learning the basics of aero engines and airframes. Then I had a further year's training at Middle Wallop in Hampshire, and came out as an aircraft technician. To cap it all, I got married, promoted to lance corporal, and posted to the Far East!

I carried on my training in Malaysia, and had a tremendous time, because I had my wife out there with me. I studied hard for my Military Certificate First Class, which you need if you want promotion. My next posting was to Berlin, as a full corporal and as a first class aircraft technician. After that I did two tours in Northern Ireland and applied for artificer training. Artificers are really a higher grade of Army mechanic – just about in the craftsman class – and it is quite difficult to get

David inspects the rotary system on a helicopter. Components have to be checked regularly to minimize the risk of an accident while in the air.

David hands a fitter a replacement gyro compass.

on a course. After various tests and interviews I was lucky enough to be accepted.

This meant going back to England yet again, and learning a lot more about man-management and administration. Then came my best posting yet – I was sent on loan to the Royal Navy, where I became a member of the mobile salvage unit. Our main job in life was repairing all rotary aircraft (helicopters, that is), worldwide, and carrying out an annual inspection of all naval, fixed-wing aircraft. I went all round the world. At one point, I was with the American Navy onboard *U.S.S. Nimitz* cruising in the Baltic, where I worked on the Tomcat fighter – that's quite an aircraft for a helicopter guy to work on!

After even more training, I was promoted to warrant officer two, and got offered this job at Wildenrath airfield. So here I am, in charge of all R.E.M.E. personnel on the flight. The role of the flight is to supply aircraft for the use of the Commander-in-Chief of B.A.O.R. and the Commander-in-Chief of R.A.F. Germany. We have four Gazelle helicopters, five pilots, and a total strength of twenty-five, of which nine are R.E.M.E. The pilots who fly the helicopters are all officers.

The helicopters clock about seventy-six flying hours every month doing various duties. They've each got a range of about three and a half hours. So it's up to the R.E.M.E. staff here to make sure that they are regularly serviced and safe to fly. An aircraft is full of items – gearboxes, radios, engines, shafts – which have to be changed after a certain time. It's all very tightly controlled, and flying hours are carefully logged. An engine, say, will last 2,000 flying hours, so just prior to that point we demand a new engine from stores, get it down here and change it ourselves when the 2,000 hours are up.

It takes about a morning to change an engine on one of these helicopters, and then about a day to do air-testing on it. A main rotor-head can take you a week, because the actual spanner-bending will take four hours, and you then have to track every individual rotor-blade and make the aircraft fly without bouncing. It's rather like balancing a wheel on a car, except that you have to keep going up, coming down again, doing a few minor adjustments and then going up in the air again. The worst thing in flying is vibration – it causes cracking, radios stop working, instruments shatter and so on – and the last thing you want is an aircraft that bounces all over the sky.

The other very important job we've got is flight servicing. Before and after every flight we carry out a hundred per cent check on things like fluid levels in the gearbox and hydraulic systems, and components that might have cracked or vibrated loose. We also have to wash the helicopters after every flight. The Rühr area of Germany where we are is very industrial and you can taste the filth in the air. You can imagine that the aircraft get caked with it. Washing them down is actually done by the Army Air Corps, not by the R.E.M.E.

I am in charge of quality control on the

David takes off in a Gazelle helicopter to check that the rotor blades are correctly adjusted.

David's crew refuel a helicopter for another flight.

In the operations room David finds out what jobs there are for the day.

equipment here, including all the tools, vehicles and fuel tanks. At least once a week I do a standards check. I go into the stores and check the tools to make sure they are serviceable and not out of date. We have a very strict code of tool control here, and at least once a day I make sure that everything is happening as it should.

As soon as an aircraft is grounded, a tool box is taken from the stores, and the number of that box is stamped on the aircraft's servicing document. We have to keep track of every tool that is used, so that nothing gets left by accident inside the engine, for example. That could be disastrous. In each tool box, apart from the tools, there are ten discs. If anyone wants a tool that isn't in the box, he goes to the store and gets it, and puts one of these discs in its place. When he's finished with that tool, he gets the disc back and returns it to the box. Then he hands the tool box in complete with ten discs. The sergeant in the store checks the box to make sure that nothing is missing. Only when the tool box is back in the store can the particular aircraft be cleared to fly again.

Now that I'm A.Q.M.S. I've got a lot of administrative work to do – although most of the paperwork is done by the chief clerk. First thing in the morning, when the crew are all here, I go into the operations room, get them up to date on the state of the helicopters, and find out what flights are planned. We don't have parades every morning. I usually have a glance round to see that the blokes are smart enough, and that the hangar is tidy. When I've got all the office business over with, I just float around making sure things are happening, and checking that all my crew are busy.

This is the first job I've had where I haven't got an excuse to get my hands dirty. But I still go out and put overalls on when I can, and do standards checks.

I've still got seven years of my twenty-two-

David supervises a pre-flight check on a Gazelle.

One of the giant tool boxes used by the helicopter maintenance team.

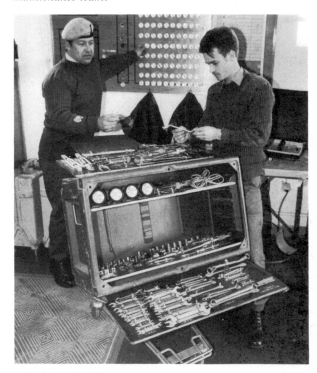

year term to do. I got my warrant after thirteen odd years, which is a bit fast, so I can't expect to go higher for a while. But I would hope to get offered a commission and become an officer, so that I can go on until I'm fifty-five, which is what I'm aiming for. I'd stay with aircraft, coming in as a lieutenant for a year, then go on to captain and hope to pick up major in the end.

I like the lifestyle here in Germany. In my spare time the family and I like going caravanning or just trekking, and we get around the country a lot. Anything to do with water I love – sub-aqua, swimming, sailing. There's a place up at Kiel where you can hire a boat for a week from the Army Yacht Club and just sail off into the Baltic. Another hobby of mine is photography, which I've practised since we were in the Far East, where equipment was so cheap.

I'd go anywhere with anyone, and I've got a wife and two girls who love travelling too. I enjoy England now and again – in fact I own a house there – but I'm not ready to settle down into a civilian life yet.

Sandy Wilson

Telecommunications technician

Sandy Wilson is 33 years old and a sergeant in the Royal Electrical and Mechanical Engineers at Düsseldorf. As a telecommunications technician he spends most of his time repairing equipment used to test Army radios.

When I left school at the age of 15 in 1964, jobs were not too difficult to come by in my home town of Glasgow. I was very fortunate – I applied for one job while I was still at school, and got it. I was an office boy in a commercial stationers, but I didn't like that much, so I moved on. From there I tried to get into a trade: I joined a firm of boilermakers as an apprentice fitter, but after a year I found that I was just being used as a tea boy and wasn't really learning a lot.

I got my driving licence and started applying for jobs as a driver. For a while I was a milkman, but what got me down there was the paperwork at the end of the day. When I was 18 I got a job in a local supermarket, working on the shop floor selling cooked meats and provisions. It was a great job and I was totally content with it – except that I could hardly live on the money they paid me. I had by now met the girl who was to become my wife, and I was looking for better pay.

It was round about then that I first came into contact with the Army. The Argyll and Sutherland Highlanders recruiting caravan came to our town all of a sudden. My wife had realized that I was interested in the Services and said, 'Why don't you go in and ask?' At this time I was twenty-four, which was a bit late for starting. Anyway, I went in and they interviewed me and told me I was too old for the Argylls, but they advised me to go into Paisley and see the recruiting officer there.

He asked me to take an I.Q. test, and told me what they could offer me – The Royal Electrical and Mechanical Engineers (R.E.M.E.) was one of the choices. At that time I was working as a builder's labourer, which was a real dead-end job. The Army offered me a trade, something that civilian life couldn't give me. At 24 years of age I was nothing – a general labourer. The Army took me in and nurtured me and gave me a kick up the backside, which was just what I needed.

I did my basic military training at Arborfield in Berkshire, where the R.E.M.E. depot is. Being selected as a technician, I was sent to the School of Electronics there, which is one of the most up-to-date electronics training establishments in Britain. I didn't do terribly well to begin with. To be quite honest, I was rather fed up – I was used to an active life and didn't like being lectured at by a bored-looking instructure. After a spell of illness I asked to be removed from the electronics side and to go to somewhere like a vehicle mechanics' course where I could work with my hands.

This is when, luckily for me, I came into contact with an American major over here on an exchange visit. When he saw my attitude he took me to one side and told me to get my finger out. He said that he would give me some direction, and I had to report to him every third day to tell him how I was getting on. With this bit of encouragement, I passed through the School of Electronics and came out as a third-class technician.

Then I went into the big world of the Army. I was posted to a R.E.M.E. service unit attached to a light armoured reconnaissance regiment. Every front-line regiment has a unit like this – they do the fighting and we make sure they've got the wheels to fight on. The unit is split into three: one part works with the soldiers in the front line, maintaining radios, vehicles and so on; behind that you've got the field workshops, and behind that are the base workshops, who actually strip equipment right down and rebuild it.

With that regiment I went on an exercise to Cyprus. It was pure soldiering, with a lot of foot-slogging. As luck would have it, the corporal in charge of my section went down with sunstroke, and I had to take over, being a lance corporal. So, very early in my Army career, I had to learn about leadership.

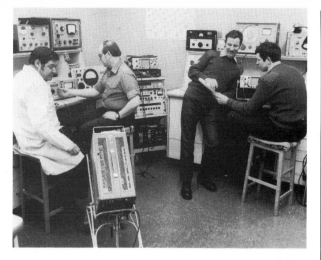

Just a few of the pieces of automatic test equipment which are used in Sandy's workshop.

Sandy examines a loose connection in a piece of test equipment.

I found it a great advantage being an older man than most of the other newly-recruited soldiers. If you're standing on the drill square with a big hairy sergeant shouting at you – for your own benefit, of course – you can understand what he's doing and it won't affect you as much as an 18-year-old boy. Also, I wasn't treated like a child to the same extent. A sergeant appreciates it if an older man pulls his weight, and the young recruits naturally come to an older recruit with their problems and so on – they look up to you.

When I was in Cyprus, I filled in a form asking for my next posting to be in the Middle East or the Far East. But when I got back to the regiment in U.K., my commanding officer came up to me and said, 'Corporal Wilson, you have asked for a Far East posting. Well, you've got as far east as you can go without

Sandy exchanges an old circuit board for a new one.

Sandy hands over a completed job card to his supervisor.

coming back on yourself – Northern Ireland!'

Belfast was a revelation to me. My wife and children came out with me, and we lived in quarters in a completely enclosed camp which was very well guarded. I never felt worried about my family, but at times I felt scared to death for myself. The Army does the very best it can for your family, and they bend over backwards to help you relax, with clubs and concerts and all that.

I was in civilian clothes most of the time, and was working on repairing the walkie-talkie radios used by the patrols. Job satisfaction there is 100 per cent – I'd even go so far as to say 110 per cent! A bloke comes up and tells you his radio is not working too well; you take it away, check it out, give it a few tweaks and give it back to him. Then after the patrol he comes back to you and says, 'It's never been better'. That's a great joy.

It's only in a situation like that when the soldier realizes that the radio is the most important piece of Army equipment he has got. It doesn't matter who's shooting at you, you can always hide behind a brick wall and radio for help.

From Northern Ireland I went back to England for my first-class course, with more advanced electronics and a higher standard of maths. Then I was posted here, which is something different again. We are called the R.E.M.E. Technical Services, and I am part of the calibration section. If you've got a radio that needs servicing or has been repaired, there are certain things that need to be tested on it – output, frequency, noise ratios and so on. So you have to have special equipment to do the testing, and my job is repairing that equipment.

As you can imagine, it is most important that the test equipment is working properly and accurately. The people who make things like radios and radar sets lay down the exact standards that their products need to be kept to. So our test equipment has to match those standards accurately. After I, or one of the other lads here, have mended it, it goes to be calibrated. If the output is supposed to be, say, one volt, then they make sure that it gives out exactly one volt.

When I started in the Army, it was all 'steam' electronics, and you used to talk about valves and transistors. But now it's all module changing, using boards with microchips. If you've got a fault, it saves time to take the old board out and send it back for repair, and just slot a new one in. They may say that the old board is not worth repairing, snap it, and chuck it in the bin. Putting in a new board is often cheaper than the time and manpower it takes to repair an old one.

At the moment, I am working with test equipment for the 'Clansman' range of radios. Because I am limited to this one range, I have really got to know it well. When I come in in the morning, there is usually some work left on my bench from the night before. I pick up the job card and see what needs to be done to the piece of equipment, switch it on and begin to look for faults. Because I know it so well, I can often put my hand on the fault straight away. Then I put it right, fill out the paper-work, and pass the job card on to my section head. After that, the equipment goes over to be calibrated.

Most of the tests I do are manual. Even complex equipment can be broken down into certain areas, just like a map, with dividers, attenuators and so on, and you just test each one at a time and isolate what is wrong.

If I want to go any higher than sergeant, I shall have to go on an artificer training course. Basically, the Army wants to find out if you can still learn. I've been in the Army now for eight years, and if I get onto the artificer course this autumn and pass it, I shall probably stay in for my full twenty-two-year term. You can sign on for three, six or nine years, with a one-year option. This means that if I want to leave after nine years, I put my notice in after eight, and serve a year's notice.

There are still a lot of places I'd like to go to with the Army – Hong Kong and Woomera, in Australia, are just two of them. But Germany's a great place too. I've just bought a tent and I'm going to go camping with my wife and two children – all the camp sites here are really first class, with all the facilities. As well as that, I'm learning canoeing.

Sandy uses some automatic test equipment to detect a fault.

Bernard 'Mac' McDonald
Rifleman

'Mac' McDonald is 28 years old. He joined the Army when he was 20 because of the promise of an exciting life. Now he is a corporal and section leader in an infantry regiment, and has had nine tours of duty in Northern Ireland. His battalion is now stationed in Germany.

'm a Manchester man born and bred. After I left school at 15, I went into an apprenticeship with a firm making ceramic tiles. But that only lasted a year, because I got dermatitis (a kind of skin disease) from handling all the cement and stuff. So I knocked that on the head and moved down to Birmingham, where I worked for B.S.A.

That was a great job. I started off as a machine operator making rifles and then moved to the motorcycle side of it, making cycle frames. It was really the best place to work in Birmingham then. B.S.A. was a family business, and they looked after their workers and paid them well. Although there was a trade union, there were very few strikes.

Unfortunately, the firm went bankrupt for various reasons in about 1970 and I was out of work. I didn't really have much idea about what I wanted to do next, but then I started watching the news on television about the British troops in Northern Ireland. That was the time that the troubles had started to flare up again, and I got really involved with watching the soldiers.

So I thought I'd go for an Army career. It was a way of getting away from the disappointments in Birmingham and having an adventurous life as well. I don't know why I'd never thought of it before, although I didn't have any relatives in the Forces who might have encouraged me. By this time I was 20 years old, so I was a bit older than the usual recruit. Looking back on it, I'd like to have joined up in boy service straight after school – I don't think I would have missed civvy life one little bit!

I went to the local Army Careers Office to join up. I did the aptitude tests and so on, and then they sent me up to the Selection Centre at Sutton Coldfield. After the tests there, they told me I could join the Lancashire Fusiliers. I knew I wanted to be an infantryman, but there was only one regiment for me – the Royal Green Jackets. They were one of the most famous regiments of all, and always seemed to be in the thick of the action in Northern Ireland.

The basic military training for an infantryman lasts for twenty-two weeks. I did mine at the depot in Winchester, and along with all the other recruits I started out with nothing and worked upwards. First of all I was issued with all my kit – uniforms, boots, hats and so on. Then I had to begin learning everything. I was trained to use weapons like self-loading rifles and sub-machine guns. They got me physically fit by sending me on runs and round assault courses. I was instructed in nuclear, biological and chemical warfare procedures. And, of course, I learned all about discipline.

During this time I often went out on exercises – night exercises, week-long exercises and others. The whole thing ended up with a week roughing it in the Brecon Beacons, where we were just dumped in the middle of nowhere and had to find our way back to base. Trust me to pick the wrong time of year – I did my training in the winter, so it was pretty nippy. Still, I enjoyed it at the time!

After my basic training I was posted straight out to Londonderry in Northern Ireland. It was like being chucked in the deep end, but after all it was that sort of thing that I'd joined the Army for. The first day, I got to our barracks out there and dropped my kit off in my quarters. That afternoon I was on patrol in the city – you can't get into the action much quicker than that.

It felt very strange and frightening at first. But I was made very welcome by the older fellows in the regiment; they gave me a lot of guidance and calmed my nerves. Each patrol is made up of four men, and is called a 'brick': the men are spaced out at the four corners of a

Mac and his men prepare to tackle an assault course during a morning exercise.

square, which is slightly at an angle so that none of them walk in a direct line with each other. There is a gap of at least thirty metres (thirty-three yards) between each man.

Often I went out on patrol up to five or six times a day, starting off at dawn and finishing up last thing at night. After each patrol I got two hours off to catch up on my sleep or have a meal. It was a pretty tiring programme, but I soon got used to it. That first tour in Northern Ireland I got shot at a couple of times – it was at the height of the troubles in 1971. But I've been back eight times since, and it's gradually got quieter.

My next posting was to Catterick, where my training continued at the depot. During

After the assault course, Mac takes his men on to the ranges. He shows one of his company the correct way to hold the rifle.

Mac often has to get up very early in the morning to go on an exercise.

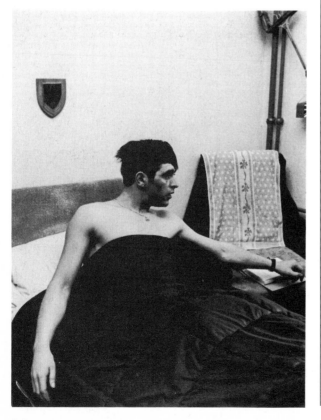

my time there I got my first stripe (lance corporal) and I also got married. As if that wasn't enough, I got selected to go on a British-Canadian expedition to Italy to climb Mont Blanc. I'd never done any climbing before, but the chance was offered to me, and it's not the sort of thing you turn down! Mont Blanc is the highest mountain in Europe, but the mountaineering training I was given by the Army was superb, and I got up with no trouble. Since then I've done a lot more climbing.

After Catterick, the battalion went out to Gibraltar (there's plenty of rock to climb there), and then came back to the depot at Tidworth in Hampshire for some more training. It was there that I got made up to full corporal. One of the best things about that stay in England was when I got posted to Winchester for a while as a training N.C.O. I was helping to train junior soldiers – youngsters who had joined up at 15 for boy service – and it was a very rewarding job. I'd love to go back into that line of work.

Now we are stationed out here in Minden, in West Germany, though not all the time. We do tours of Northern Ireland every few years, which last eighteen months or two year. That's become almost like a routine job, and there's not the same thrill there. At the moment we're waiting to go out to Canada for a month's training. Our spell out here finishes in 1986.

The Royal Green Jackets is a very special regiment. It started off as a force of mercenary soldiers got together by the British to fight the American guerrillas in their War of Independence in 1776. They taught the Army to fight in the woods by wearing green jackets, which were much better camouflage than their usual red ones.

Over here in Minden, we are part of the NATO forces who are countering the threat from the countries on the other side of the Iron Curtain. This battalion is made up with mobile units, and my particular job is being in charge of an eight-man section of riflemen. Each section travels in an armoured personnel carrier (A.P.C.), which is a tracked vehicle rather like a small tank without a turret.

We're always training in one way or another. We get up at 6 o'clock and go on parade at 8, and after that get on with whatever programme of training we're doing. If it's rifle practice, my section will draw rifles from the armoury and go down to the ranges. Fitness is also a very important part of an infantryman's life, so we try and get in two three-mile runs every day, or a circuit of the assault course, or a work-out in the gym.

Obviously, a rifleman has got to know all about his weapon – how to handle it, aim it, clean it and maintain it. But he also has to have a basic knowledge of looking after his vehicle. One of the section is the driver, so he does most of the routine checks. The actual repair work is done by a R.E.M.E. detachment stationed with our battalion – but we still have to spot anything that's wrong.

We do get a lot of sitting about sometimes, which gets a bit boring. The lads look forward to being away from the barracks on exercises, which can vary from a day on the local exercise area doing map-reading to a full-scale battalion exercise at Soltau.

On a big exercise, we drive the A.P.C. right down to the training area and get together in platoons or companies. My section can be part of a battalion advance, in which the riflemen go forward in their vehicles supported by tanks and mortar fire. When we deploy from the A.P.C., the driver and the gunner stays behind, giving us covering fire with the weapon mounted on the vehicle.

Every infantryman goes into the Army hoping for some action. There is always the pos-

Every morning the sergeant-major inspects Mac's men and makes sure that they are clean and smart.

There is no shortage of sports facilities in the Army. Mac practises his boxing on the gymnasium punchbag.

sibility of going into war at the back of your mind – otherwise you couldn't take the training seriously. Being a corporal in charge of a section I would be in thick of it. That is why, although I would obviously like to be promoted, I wouldn't like to get so high that I did more administration than real soldiering.

I'm certainly going to stay on for my full twenty-two year term, and I shall be sad when I have to leave. I don't really know what I shall do in civvy street. I may join the police force, or perhaps run a little shop specializing in the sale of weapons – that way, I won't be too far away from it.

Mac on an exercise in an A.P.C.

Jacqui Marshall

Medical assistant

Jacqui Marshall is 21. She first joined the Army at 16, but left after only two weeks! Later she tried again and qualified as a medical assistant. She now works at a medical reception centre near Düsseldorf.

I'd always taken an interest in nursing, and I thought that was the career I'd take up. Before I had left school in Hampshire I managed to get myself a job working in a convalescent home for old people, near where I live. But I only lasted a couple of weeks there, because I was only 16, straight out of school, and I found looking after old people too difficult to handle.

So I left, and went to work as a shop assistant – first in a newsagent's, then in a pet shop. I enjoyed this immensely: I love meeting people, and I'd hate to be working by myself. But then I started thinking about joining the Army, so I went to the careers office.

I hadn't completely given up the idea of nursing, although my experiences in the old people's home had put me off for a while. I had six C.S.E.s and two 'O' levels, which was enough to become a nurse, but I wanted to be able to travel, and have a secure future. Also, I had two brothers who have been in the Royal Artillery. Actually they were both totally against me joining the Army. 'Our sister isn't going into the WRAC!' they said.

That didn't stop me, because right from the start, I knew there was only one trade I was interested in, and that was medical assistant. From what the recruiting sergeant said, it seemed to be everything I wanted – just a basic training course to qualify you in nursing and clinical procedures, and not a long drawn-out two or three years with exams at the end of them. That was ideal for me, because I thought that I could get the experience later on when I was actually working.

I passed all the medical and I.Q. tests, and I was just about to go to the personnel selection officer (who decides what trade you can do), when suddenly I thought I might be doing the wrong thing and cancelled the appointment. I was really crazy and mixed up then, but the recruitment officer was very understanding and told me to leave it for a while and see how I felt.

So I waited for six months and then tried again. This time I went through all the interviews and tests again, and to the personnel selection officer, and got the trade I wanted straight off. I was put on a waiting list and, at 16 years old, I went off to the WRAC barracks at Guildford.

I spent all of two weeks there! I wasn't in the right state of mind at all. I didn't know where I was; I didn't know any of the other girls; I was terribly homesick, and I stopped eating. So straightaway I asked for a discharge and ended up going home. The first thing my father said when he met me at the station was, 'Don't you dare tell me in six months' time that you want to go back into the Army!'

Of course, as soon as I got home I calmed down and felt better, and I was really full of all the things I had done in my two weeks. My parents got sick of me talking about the course! I began to realize that it was bound to be strange for the first few weeks, and that once I got to know the girls and find my feet I would enjoy it.

I got myself a job quite quickly working as a telephonist and telex operator. But once I began to look at the situation sensibly I knew that I had done completely the wrong thing. Being in the Army was really what I wanted. I left it for a while and then broke the news to my parents. I got in touch with the recruiting sergeant again and had a chat with her. She said that in her whole career she'd never had a girl who wanted to re-enlist after giving up the course.

I had to wait six months, so I got a job in a local hospital as an auxiliary in the operating theatre. Then I went through all the interviews and everything again, and eventually got a letter telling me to report to Guildford

Jacqui gives a polio vaccination to a soldier.

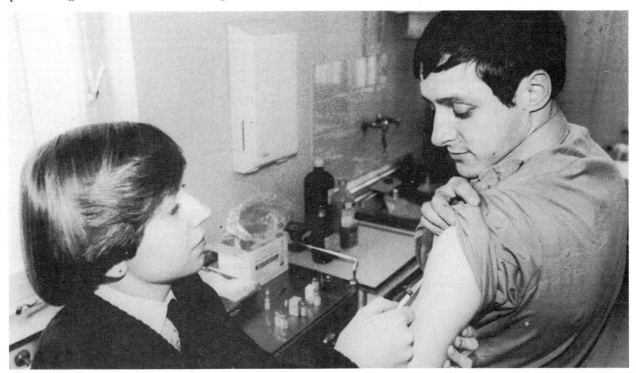

for training. This time I went in completely the right frame of mind, and thoroughly enjoyed every minute of it.

We did six weeks' basic training, which is mainly about learning discipline – not just saluting and marching, but learning to live with others in a small space. I went straight off after that to my trade training at Aldershot. There are about thirty different trades a WRAC can do now, including draughtswoman, driver, cook and military police. There are WRACs training in the R.E.M.E. as mechanics of different sorts, and also in the Royal Corps of Transport.

We are also doing weapon training now, and I think they have added it to the basic training course. It's a very good idea from a defence point of view. In wartime, the men can go off and do the fighting and we can stay and guard the unit without having to keep men out of the front line to look after us. Don't get me wrong; I don't think girls should be armed, but we should be able to handle weapons just in case we ever need to. To be honest, most of the girls find weapons like the S.M.G. (sub-machine gun) a bit heavy to use.

I did four weeks' medical training, which is basic first aid teaching and learning clinical procedures for working in the wards. You learn how to take blood pressures, temperatures, pulses and so on; how to read prescriptions, do bandaging and lay up medical trays. After that, there are three days of exams, followed by a week in a military hospital getting practical experience. If you want to do any more detailed medical training, to be a dental hygienist or an S.R.N., you really have to join the Queen Alexandra Royal Army Nursing Corps to start off with.

My first posting was to London, where I was attached to the Royal Military Police. I was working at the Hyde Park Barracks. That was an excellent first job, because I was using

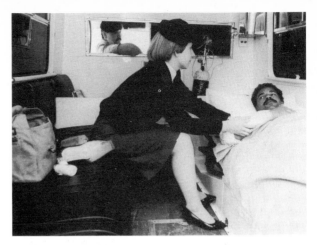

When there is an emergency call, Jacqui goes out in an ambulance to look after the patient.

Jacqui tests a patient's blood pressure.

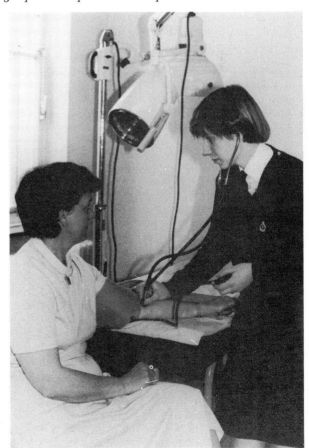

everything that I had been trained for, from clerical work to dispensing medicines. It built up my confidence, but after only three months the opportunity came up to work out here at Rheindahlen.

The medical reception centre on this camp is open to all military personnel within the vicinity – all the troops and officers and their families, plus the British civilians such as teachers and clerks. It is run by a senior medical officer, and under him are eight medical officers (M.O.s). The centre works rather like an ordinary doctor's surgery, except of course that we're dealing with soldiers. We have to do their medical gradings, and give them medical tests before they go on courses. Apart from that, we have a family planning clinic and ante-natal classes, and a lot of injections to give people. All this is on top of the usual surgery.

First thing in the morning, at 8.15, we have sick parade, when the soldiers are seen by the

Jacqui files medical records so that they can be found easily when a patient next visits the centre.

The medical reception centre has its own dispensary. Jacqui has brought in a prescription to be made up.

M.O.s. They send the fit ones back to work and the sick ones to hospital or to bed in their barracks. Next we see the N.C.O.s, who can make appointments, and after them the officers, soldiers' families and civilians. All this time I am busy in the reception office booking appointments. After lunch, there is a regular programme of injections and special clinics.

I have to work a six-day week every other week, and sometimes that can be pretty hectic, as well as tiring. Last week, for example, I was here for twenty-four hours on Monday – which meant sleeping the night here and being on call for emergencies. Even if I get no sleep I have to be ready for work at 8.15 the next day. Wednesday was another twenty-four hour shift, as well as Saturday. I got the Sunday off!

If there is an emergency call, I go out in the ambulance with the driver. These are usually traffic accidents, or a soldier injured during training. Once I had to take a diabetic to hospital; he was a big man, who was having a fit, and we needed two men just to hold him down. For temporary cases, we have got two small wards in the centre itself where patients can stay for a short time.

This trade isn't very good in terms of promotion. I'm a lance corporal now, and due for promotion to full corporal, which is not bad going because I've only been in the WRAC for three years. But getting to sergeant will be a different matter, because there are only two sergeants who are WRAC medics in the whole Army.

In any case, I may have to leave the Army in the next few years. I have just got married to a military policeman, who has been posted to Northern Ireland. Very luckily I managed to get a posting nearby, so we shall be off there for two years soon. But I shan't always be able to do that. You've got to accept the fact that if you can't get a posting near your husband, you're going to have to leave the Army. They do their best to post married couples together, but with a medical assistant it's very difficult, as we are only stationed in England, Northern Ireland and Germany.

I shall stay in as long as I can – I'm really beginning to enjoy life in the Army. I feel that if I leave now I shall be looking back all the time at the things I didn't do. So in the next three or four years I've got to pack in all the ski-ing, parachuting and other excitements that I possibly can.

The medical reception centre deals with soldiers and their wives and children. Jacqui often lends a hand in the waiting room.

Phil Fionda
Cook

Nineteen-year-old Phil Fionda decided to become a chef soon after he left school. He now works in a cookhouse on the Joint Headquarters camp at Rheindahlen, near Düsseldorf.

I wasn't particularly bright at anything at school in Bristol except for home economics and drama. The first thing I really wanted to do was stage lighting in the theatre. I wasn't too interested in catering then – it was just a bit of fun when we used to throw pastry round the classroom. Every other exam I took I failed abysmally on.

While I was at school we were taken on careers trips to find out what jobs were like. I went to the Bristol Old Vic theatre and had a chat to the guy that does the stage lighting there. He told me that he'd been there for ten years and had spent most of his time working his way up from the bottom, sweeping the stage and making cups of tea. That put me off, because I wanted to get straight into a job and learn it. So I decided to give up that idea.

I sat down and thought, 'What else am I good at?' The only other thing was home economics, and I decided to be a chef. I went round a few hotels on careers trips with the school and liked what I saw, so I applied for a couple of jobs as a commis chef (apprentice chef). But at first I had no joy, so I did the next best thing and went to work in an iron-mongery shop that sold heavy-duty catering equipment, such as deep-fat fryers.

I worked there for about six months after I left school and then I actually got a job as a commis chef at a hotel in Bristol. My official hours were from nine o'clock until two, and from six in the evening until ten at night. But what happened in practice was that I would go in at eight o'clock to help with the breakfasts, prepare vegetables for lunch until about two, and then go into the bar and help the barman change the barrels and all the rest of it. After that it was making beds and cleaning floors and back into the kitchen in the evenings – all on £30 a week.

In fact, all the people I know who've started out as commis chefs have done everything in the hotel except work in the kitchen. I was also supposed to be going on day release to college for my City and Guilds certificate, but although the manager kept on promising, I never went. Soon I was really hacked off with the job and wanted to get out.

I still wanted to be a chef, and at this time I didn't have any inclination to join the Army at all. But then the Army Catering Corps (A.C.C.) display team came to Bristol. I had a look at what they were doing and was quite impressed, so I went down to the Army Careers Office and had a chat with the guy there. Over the next three weeks I didn't give it too much thought, but I must somehow have made the decision. I simply went in and signed up and that was it – I hardly even asked any questions.

So there I was at 17, an Army chef apprentice. I did my basic military training at the Army Catering Corps depot at Aldershot. Discipline was the word – training from six o'clock in the morning until eight at night

Phil carries in a load of potatoes.

The soldiers who eat in Phil's cookhouse are of many nationalities including, Dutch, German and Belgian.

doing 15-km (10-mile) runs, bulling your boots, yes sir, no sir and all that.

Then I had twenty-two weeks of trade training. I started off learning all about pastry – making fancy cakes and so on – and after a couple of weeks of that I was tested to see if I was up to standard. Next I went to the kitchen and did basic foods like braised beef and roast lamb, and have another trade test. From there I did larder work, which is preparing things such as mayonnaise and pork pies.

Eventually I was put in the kitchens downstairs where I did the cooking for the rest of the recruits for two weeks, and put into practice what I had learned upstairs. I soon found it didn't fit, because instead of cooking for myself I now had to cook for two hundred people! That's how it goes on; you do cooking for the ordinary soldiers, in the officers' mess and the sergeants' mess. At the end of it you have your B2 Army qualification, and your City and Guilds certificate, which I think is a fairly difficult exam to pass.

I actually stayed at Aldershot for about eight months, because I got into the shooting team. We went in for various Army competitions and I was kept back for a bit just so that I could stay in the team. That was a lot of fun.

Then I came out here. This is a NATO unit, which means that I'm working with Dutch, Germans and Belgians, and the type of food is very different from what you would get in an British cookhouse. We use a lot of convenience foods here, things like gravy powder and soup powder which aren't used in the British Army. That's not really cooking – you're not a *chef de cuisine*, you're a 'chef de packet!' It is also means that I'm not learning as much as I would in a regular cookhouse.

I do a six-hour day here – in a normal British unit I'd probably do twice that. At the moment I'm on the middle shift, which means that I come in at about 8.30 in the morning. I look at the big blackboard which has the menu of the day written on it, and see which jobs I've been allotted to do.

Today, for example, I had to do fish in batter, chicken paprika and braised steak. First of all I decided which one was going to take the longest, and started straightaway making the batter for the fish. I put that in the fridge, got the fish out of the freezer and thawed it out, cut up all the meat for lunch, started my braised beef off and put it in the oven. Then I sat down for half an hour and had a cup of tea and a chat with a mate of mine. After lunch was finished, I had to get on and prepare the tea, before knocking off at about five o'clock.

On other shifts you have to cook breakfast, or serve lunch and tea, or be preparing pastries and cakes for lunch. Altogether we are cooking for about 180 people, which generally means there is some food left over, and that can always get used the next day.

Hygiene is very important, and we clean as we work. There is one catering inspection every year, when an A.C.C. officer comes round to make sure that all the equipment is in order and that we're not working in dirty or dangerous conditions. Other than that, we

Phil chops up apples for lunch.

are very careful to keep the kitchen clean, because of the danger of rats and mice and cockroaches. This one is a very clean kitchen.

English cookhouses are very hot on cleanliness, because a lot of their equipment is out of date and has to be kept in good condition. Sometimes you can have six cooks on duty – three of them will be cooking, and the others will be cleaning up!

Next month, I'm being posted just down the road to another company, where there's proper English cooking. I shall learn a lot

The rules on hygiene are very strict in an Army cookhouse. Phil carefully cleans out a boiler.

more there. I was a bit afraid of being sent to an infantry regiment, where you really can get hammered. You have to be a good cook and go out on exercises with the troops. You dig a trench and put your cookers in it, and you're working from six in the morning until twelve at night, every day.

I hate exercises. But if you think about it, it's only fair that we should have such long hours, because we've got the cookers to cuddle up to and keep us warm, and in the kitchens you never go hungry or thirsty. When you think about guys in the infantry who might be up to their necks in mud trying to get a vehicle out of a trench, you say to yourself, 'Would I like to be doing that?' That way, you learn to take the rough with the smooth.

My first three-year term is just coming to an end, and I'm signing on for another three. I've got a posting to the U.K. coming up, for a course at the Army Apprentice College at Chepstow. I'm really looking forward to that because it is quite near to Bristol, and I'll be able to see my mates.

To be honest, I don't like Germany, although I like driving round Europe, and by car from here you can easily get to Holland,

Phil puts the finishing touches on to a cake.

Phil listens to one of his favourite records in his room after a hard day's work in the cookhouse.

Belgium, Switzerland and Austria. If I was offered a post in Cyprus, I'd think about it, but I don't really like hot places – even here it's murder in the summer.

Outside work, my whole life revolves around music. I usually buy about four record albums a weeks, and I sing in a rhythm and blues band. We do the mess circuit of officers' messes and sergeants' messes. The music we have to play is chart rubbish mainly, for dancing, but the money is good. For enjoyment we go out on the Dutch and German circuits and play what we like – we have a good time, but we get paid very little.

It's difficult to look ahead. In another three years I shall have had an awful lot more experience of catering, as well as doing my course at Chepstow. I shall be far better trained than anyone who has worked in a hotel for the same amount of time. If I leave the Army, it should be easy for me to get a job as a chef in civvy street. That's partly because people think it's such a horrible occupation – it's filthy, it's hot and the money's rubbish – and nobody knows why we do it! My ultimate ambition is to run a restaurant – probably a club specializing in good English food.

Keith Goldie
Radio relay operator

Keith Goldie is 21 years old. He joined the Army for an adventurous life and trained as a combat radioman. He is now stationed with the Royal Signals in Germany and is a radio relay operator.

I wasn't very bright in science subjects at school. I'd never really been interested in radios or electronics either, so it's rather surprising that I am now in the Royal Signals, working with radios.

The main reason why I joined the Army was not so much to learn a trade but to have an adventurous life. When I left grammar school in Kent, I worked in a supermarket for a while, and then got a job in a factory doing sheet metal work. Being indoors all the time made me very fed-up, and I knew I just had to find something that would get me some fresh air and adventure.

At school, I'd thought about joining the Navy, but I didn't get in because I didn't have any C.S.E.s or 'O' levels or anything (I did get two 'O' levels in the end, but it was too late then). So, when I'd just gone 17, I signed up for the Royal Signals in what they call man service – if you're younger, you have to start in boy service.

I went to the depot at Catterick to do ten weeks of basic military training. It was very hard; I was up at 5.30 in the morning cleaning out the dormitory block before going to breakfast. After that, I had to go back to the block to make sure it was clean again! Then I was out working really hard through the day, doing drill, P.T. and everything.

Before that course was finished, they took me to the personnel selection office and helped me to decide which trade I wanted to do. It was largely my own choice, of course, but they tried to steer me to where they've got lots of vacancies. I said to the recruiting officer that I'd like to do any trade working with radios. I decided that on the spur of the moment – I only knew that I didn't fancy being a mechanic or anything like that. So I ended up being a combat radioman.

My trade training course lasted eleven weeks in all, because every signaller is taught to drive as well as learning his trade. It was all very different to the basic training – I didn't have to get up so early in the morning, and I had civvies to clean the block for me!

On the course, I was taught the basics of radios, and electrics generally. I started off learning electrical safety – how to wire a plug, how to mend fuses, how to earth equipment and how to get people away from an electrical fire. Then I learned how to connect cables together, using either special tools or my bare hands; how to use batteries in series and in parallel; and how to look after them. Generators are very important to a mobile team, so we were trained in checking them and using them correctly.

Being in the Signals, I had to learn a lot about voice procedure and discipline over the air. I had to remember the correct words to use, and how to take turns at talking so that people aren't butting in all the time.

The radio side of the training was pretty hard, I thought. One of the most difficult things is learning how to tune a radio in. It's not like turning on a transistor radio and finding the right station – you've got a whole range of meters to watch and make sure you get the correct readings. Some radios can take up to half an hour to tune in properly.

I came out here to Germany as a signaller, for my first posting. Really, it was like being thrown into the deep end. At the depot, I was taught everything in a classroom, but here I was stuck in a wagon with all the kit in it and I had to get a grip of myself, remember everything I'd learned and put it into practice. I soon picked up the things which you had to know, but which they didn't teach me during my training – little tricks and techniques

Keith tunes up a long-distance transmitter. Fine tuning of some radios can take up to half an hour.

Keith unwinds the cable for a radio mast from a drum. Then he connects the cable to the mast before pumping it up.

which are very useful indeed.

Although I trained as a combat radioman, my particular trade is now being split into two, and we've got a choice of becoming either a radio operator or a radio relay operator. I chose to work in radio relay, which means that I am a link in a chain of radio signals in the field.

The radio is one of the most important pieces of equipment that a soldier uses today. When a unit is up in the front line, it can keep in touch with its base – send back information about troop movements, receive new orders, call up reinforcements and so on. But a portable radio signal is only effective up to a certain distance. The job of a radio relay is to increase that range.

I'm in a two-man detachment with a corporal, and we have a truck with two radio masts, two radios and a generator. On exercises, we would station our truck as we were directed, preferably hidden in a wood and on top of a hill. We pump up the masts and tune in the radio sets – one in contact with the base, and the other in contact with the front line. There can be a whole chain of relay points between the two, depending on how far they are apart. We don't actually have to do any talking, except to make sure that we can get in touch with both parties if we need to, and that they can talk to each other.

Sometimes we could be moving our position once or twice a day; other times we can be stuck in that wood for three days and more. The truck is all cammed up (camouflaged) with netting and scrim, and we take it in turns to do shifts by the radios.

Because we're stationary for such long periods, we can take out a lot of home comforts. There's the vehicle to sit in, for a start, and a little tent which fixes on the side of it for sleeping quarters. The truck contains its own table, chairs, cookers and pots and pans, and we're issued with compo rations to cook up. We can take along a television or a radio and make another aerial for them.

Altogether, we get it quite easy if we're not moving about too much. The one piece of action is the stand-to in the morning, when we run out to our trench and take up a defensive position, as if the enemy were attacking.

But most of the time we stay at squadron headquarters and have a regular five-day week. We go on parade at 8.15 – although twice a week we have to do P.T., starting at 7.30 (we're the fittest squadron in the regiment). On parade we are inspected to make sure we're neat and tidy enough, and then told what our jobs are for the day by the staff sergeant.

Usually, this means doing maintenance work on our vehicles, cleaning them, checking underneath them and making sure that everything's in order. We are always getting inspections to see that our equipment is up to standard for exercises. If you find anything that needs fixing, you write out a form for the

The masts on the radio truck are pumped using air pressure from the truck's braking system.

Once the mast is in position Keith can check the radio.

R.E.M.E. detachment – we don't do the repairs ourselves, we just find them before somebody else does and we get into trouble for it! All our repairs are done by R.E.M.E. technicians, both on the vehicle and on the radio equipment.

So, as well as checking our vehicles, we go over our radio gear to see that it's working. We get the generators connected up, make sure the truck is earthed, switch on the sets and pump up the masts. The masts are pushed up by the air pressure used for the truck's brakes, so we have to be careful that there are no leaks.

This regular maintenance and cleaning up, along with any other routine jobs you may be given, takes up the average day. At 4.30 I knock off, unless I'm on guard duty. I have to do this three or four times a month, and it means getting dressed in combat gear and reporting to the guard room after normal working hours. I mount guard at six o'clock, and I have to prowl around, keeping an eye on the gate and the perimeter of the camp and checking security, until 7 the next morning. After that I have to go straight on to work at 8 o'clock if it's a weekday.

Later this year I'm being posted to Herford, which is just up the road. I've been told that it's a lot easier to get promoted there, because there aren't too many full corporals blocking the way. Once I get one stripe up (become a lance corporal), I can start going on courses which will give me a wider training. As it is, I'm soon going on an upgrading course which will take me to the the top of my particular trade – a B1 signaller. It will also take me on to a higher pay scale.

I signed on originally for three years, and I didn't bother signing off when that time was up, which means that I can do my full twenty-two or just put in a year's notice when I feel like getting out. I'm quite happy with that

arrangement. If the Army ever gets on top of me – which I don't think is likely – that's what I should do.

Besides, looking at the situation at the moment, I'm much better off in the Army. There's not very much I can do with this trade in civvy street, because it is special to the Army. They use radios in the Post Office, for example, but to operate those you've got to be a technician so that you can use them and repair them. If all else fails, I've always got my H.G.V. licence.

The Army's got into my blood, too. In my spare time I like building models of military aircraft and vehicles, and reading books on Army history. Finding out about the blunders that were made in the past gives you a new outlook on service life!

Keith and the other signalmen are inspected every morning to make sure that their uniforms are tidy.

Neil Corless
Supply clerk

Neil Corless is 30 years old. He joined the Army as soon as he left school at 15. He is now a supply clerk at a huge Army Ordnance depot dealing with motor spares for all Army vehicles.

The first time I lived in the U.K. was when I was 14 years old. Before that, my family had been moving round the world with my father, who was a soldier in what was then called the Royal Army Service Corps (later split into the Corps of Transport and the Ordnance Corps, which I joined). I was actually born in Ismailia in Egypt, and as a child I lived in Malaya, Singapore, Cyprus, Kenya, Aden and a few other places as well.

This meant that I only had about eighteen months of schooling in England, and I left school at the earliest possible age – 15 – with no G.C.E.s or C.S.E.s. My ambition had always been to become a vet and work with animals, but without the certificates, there was no hope of that. So I went straight into the Army. At the time I had to, because my father had just died, and the family had to be sorted out.

I started off in boy service, because I was so young. This is an advantage in many ways, because I had a chance of sitting for the three stages of the Army Certificate of Education. The normal soldier who joins at 17 or over has to wait until he joins his regiment before doing that. I also learned the routine of Army life – drill, exercises, sport and so on – and altogether it was a very interesting couple of years.

After that, I went on to my trade training at Camberley. The trade of clerk was decided for me, really, because I had the right education, and because they had vacancies there. The supply clerk's course lasted four weeks, and I learned all about the various functions, from issuing boots and socks to typing and basic computer work. At that time, nearly all our work was manual – the counting of pieces of equipment and the paperwork – but nowadays, of course, it's all on computer.

My first posting was to Chilwell, where the provision branch of the Ordnance Corps is

Neil supervises the storing of vehicle tyres. The workmen are all German civilians.

Neil checks the location of certain items with a shed storeman.

stationed. That was fairly humdrum work, mostly dealing with contracts between the Army and civilian supply firms. But soon I was sent out with an Ordnance detachment to join the United Nations peacekeeping force in Cyprus – that was more like it.

In Cyprus, we were responsible for issuing everything that the Army needed – that is the real function of the Royal Army Ordnance Corps (R.O.A.C.). Barbed wire, engine spares, toilet paper – you name it, we supply it. The most interesting part of it was what is called the Turkish rotation. At that time, the Turkish Armies in Cyprus were swapped round every year, and we had to control the issuing of every single item to the incoming troops. It included everything, from putting up tents on the dock and supplying paper plates to providing silver cutlery for the officers' messes. Everything had to be accounted for, down to the last spoon – and that's a lot of paperwork.

My next job abroad was different again. I was sent to an aircraft workshop in Celle, Germany, for three and a half years. It was a good place for a supply clerk to be, because I was in the stores section dealing with all the aircraft spares, and was actually in physical contact with the parts themselves. Most of the clerks I've known like to do their work manually. Today, when nearly everything is on the computer, it's lost a lot of the magic – you can sit in an office all day in front of the computer print-out, and never see what you're dealing with at all.

When I came back to the U.K., I did a tour of Northern Ireland, supplying mechanical spares for the R.E.M.E. workshops, and was then posted out here to Germany again. At this depot we store M.T. (motor transport) spares for the whole of the British Army of the Rhine – that includes tyres, complete engines, parts of engines, clutch linings, fuel tanks and anything else you can think of that an Army vehicle needs, from a Chieftain tank to a Cortina staff car. We also store adventure training equipment here – things like canoes, tents and skis.

My job is to make sure that the flow of supplies keeps going. We're responsible first of all for finding out what each unit is demanding: it might be an engine for a tank, for example. If a unit in the field needs a new engine, it puts in a demand form to the nearest Ordnance depot. If that depot hasn't got the right engine, the demand will be put on to the computer and will be sent to all the other depots until one is found.

There are Ordnance supply clerks at every depot dealing with these demands, and making sure the items get issued to the correct unit. The central computer point for Germany is at Viersen, and if something can't be found here, the demand goes over to the main depot in the U.K., which is at Bicester. If there are none of the correct spares to be

All information about Ordance stores is filed on computer. Neil checks the quantities of a certain component.

As a supply clerk and a staff sergeant, Neil always has a lot of desk work to do.

found anywhere, a new consignment will be ordered from the civilian contractors.

Obviously, some demands are more important that others, and we have a special system of priority. If a unit in battle, say, has a tank that cannot work without a vital spare part, then that is a very urgent demand. We give it a red star, and call it 'priority one – war footing'; it has to be out of the depot within two hours. At the other end of the scale is 'priority fifteen', which covers routine, everyday issues. One of my jobs is to visit the sheds regularly and make certain that everything is getting sent out by its target date.

At the moment I'm not actually involved with the stores themselves. It's the men from sergeant downwards who do all the nitty-gritty of supplying. Staff sergeants like myself, and warrant officers, oversee it all and ensure that the flow of supplies is going smoothly.

My job is in planning, which I think is just an adult word for dogsbody! I have to cover everything from people coming to visit the depot to what is called works services. This is any sort of work to do with the maintenance of the depot itself. For example, this afternoon I've got to go right round the depot with my boss and find out where we need trees to be planted.

In fact, the term 'supply clerk' doesn't really cover the range of things that we have to do. One day we could be sitting in front of a computer, and another we could be out measuring railway lines. We have to control all the paperwork for supply and demand from beginning to end, and if we're out on a field exercise, we have to manhandle the stores ourselves as well.

The way it's heading now, everything is going computer-mad. When I first came into the Corps, I enjoyed the job tremendously. It was a fun thing, and everybody was happy to stay at the same rank if they had to. That was why I liked working in the aircraft workshops so much – I could see the aircraft, I could see the stores, and I was part of the action. I even knew the people in the U.K. that I was getting the stores from. You could do much the same job as you do now – sometimes do it a bit quicker – and have a laugh about it.

Now, on the other hand, I'm just a cog in a machine. The equipment that we have to deal with is a lot more technical and high-powered, and they're looking for a better-qualified class of soldier to join the Corps. In my early days the recruits who weren't up to scratch for a technical job in, say, the R.E.M.E., were told to go into the R.A.O.C. But today they are only selecting recruits with G.C.E.s, and the ordinary soldier can't get in.

The number of supply clerks has also fallen dramatically since the introduction of computers and the cuts in government defence spending. When I was first at Chilwell, there were fifty clerks there, and now there are only ten. But all this doesn't really bother me too much. Servicemen who have been in the

Neil makes sure that a red star priority order goes out on time – that means, within two hours.

Part of Neil's job is to look after maintenance of the rail depot.

Army for a while soon learn to adapt to new surroundings and new types of job.

I've still got nine years to go before I complete my twenty-two. The next step is up to warrant officer, and then there's more chance of me being sent farther afield, to places such as Cyprus and Hong Kong. It's also possible that I may go on loan service to the armies in Brunei or Kuwait. That would be a terrific job – not to say a very lucrative one – because when you're on loan you get paid at their rates, and all sorts of perks as well. I would have to depend on local resources for my supplies. I'd probably get the chance to do a bit of teaching while I was there too.

When I come out of the Army, I honestly don't know what I'll want to do. What I would probably be best at would be controlling the movement of pieces of equipment inside a large workshop – such as a motor wholesalers or a warehouse.

In the meantime, though, I'm enjoying being in Germany. My wife and I have got two children who have just got to the age when they can enjoy travelling around Europe, and this is an ideal base to start from if you want to get to Holland, Belgium, France or even Switzerland. The only trouble is that I'm a fanatical golfer, and the nearest golf course is two hours' drive away at Brugen, so every weekend I jump in my car and I'm away. My handicap is fourteen at the moment, but I hope by next week it will be better than that.

Bob Price
Field surveyor

Bob Price is 24 years old. He has been in the Army for three years and is now a field surveyor with a topographical squadron in Germany, where he helps to provide ground points for new military maps.

When I was younger there were lots of different things I wanted to be – an actor, a sailor, and even an archaeologist. But when I actually came to take my 'O' levels at school I had run out of ideas. I got eight 'O' levels, and went on to take 'A' levels – maths, which I passed, and physics, which I failed. Obviously, after that I couldn't go on to university and get a degree.

I should really have stayed on and re-sat my physics exam, but the trouble was I had itchy feet. My father had been in the Army, and as a result our family had tended to travel about quite a bit. I was born in Yorkshire, but we didn't stay there very long, moving to different places around the world until my father retired and settled in his home town in South Wales.

So I had got used to the Army way of life, and had this urge to be moving on. Rather than stay on at school, get another 'A' level and do a degree, I went straight on to the Polytechnic of Wales to do an H.N.D. course in Civil Engineering. It was a sandwich course, and I learned all about things like building roads and bridges, water mechanics and dam-construction, stresses and strains in materials, surveying and technical drawing.

During the summer vacations I used to work with local civil engineering firms, and because of this experience I began to get an idea of what sort of job I would be ending up doing – and I wasn't too happy with it! From what I could see, I would probably be a site agent, who is in charge of work on the site: he has a lot of responsibility but not much money. There was some trouble on one of the sites I worked on – the firm were behind time with the contract, some labourers went on strike, and the site agent was getting a lot of hassle from his superiors. Personally, I was glad to get away from there.

All the same, when my course finished, I

knew I had to get a job. My experience with civvy firms had put me off working for them, but I obviously had to find something that would use the knowledge I had gained at the polytechnic. I'd sometimes toyed with the idea of following in my father's footsteps and going into the Army, so I made a few inquiries, and the trade of field surveyor seemed to suit me best. I went up to the Army Selection Centre at Sutton Coldfield, where you do aptitude tests so that they can work out what trade you're best suited for.

I joined up on my twenty-first birthday. At first, I was told that I was too old to get into field survey, and would have to go to the Army Apprentice College at Chepstow. But after starting my basic military training as a design draughtsman, I was unhappy with it, and managed to get myself on a field survey course. In fact, there was a six-month gap after my basic training, so I went over there to gain a bit of background experience, and to let the Army see that I was suited to it.

Back in England, I went to the School of Military Survey at Hermitage in Berkshire for what is called the Tec 3 course – that is the first step of qualification in field survey. As I get better qualified, I shall become a Tec 2 and then, I hope, a Tec 1.

The course was supposed to last six months. In fact, we were there for seven, because the Queen was coming to open the school officially, and we stayed behind for an extra month. I learned a lot that was new, although of course I already knew a lot about the actual survey work – using instruments for measuring angles and distances – from my time at polytechnic. When the training was over, I was posted straight out here to Germany, to work with a topographical squadron.

There are several reasons why I'm glad I came into the Army so late. For a start, I'd

Bob takes a height reading using his theodolite.

Bob directs the positioning of the banderole, or marker pole, on which he will sight his theodolite to take the height reading.

Above *Bob marks new features on a map by plotting his readings on to a transparent overlay.*

already learned a lot of the technical stuff when I was doing my 'A' levels and my H.N.D. course – things like engineering drawing and using theodolites. Since I've been a soldier, I've never had time to further my education – I'm never in one place long enough. Another advantage is that you're a lot more mature at 21 than you are at 17, and you've found out what adult life in civvy street is really like. I think that having my H.N.D. qualification certainly helped me to get my first stripe more quickly.

The basic job of a field surveyor is to help in the production of maps which are used by units out in the field. We go out with our instruments and measure distances, angles and heights of certain points on the ground.

We use three main instruments. The first, and most well-known, is a theodolite, which is used for measuring horizontal and vertical angles by lining it up with a specially calibrated pole called a banderole. For finding out distances, we usually use an Aga 14. You set

Below *Bob measures distance using an Aga 14*

this up at one point, and line up a prism at the other. The Aga sends out a light beam, which hits the prism and is reflected back, so by knowing the speed of the beam and measuring the time it takes to travel there and back you can work out the distance.

Another way of measuring distances is with the tellurometer. This uses radio waves instead of light, and the process takes a lot longer. The advantage of this instrument is that it will measure much longer distances: an Aga will go up to 14 km (9 miles) on a fine day, but a tellurometer has been used over 100 km (60 miles). And, because it operates on radio waves, you can talk to the person at the other end. For the kind of work we do out here, the Aga is the most suitable.

With these instruments, we plot and co-ordinate points on the ground. Our information is then given to the air surveyor, who uses it in conjunction with a series of aerial photographs to produce a map.

That is the main job of a field surveyor. But over here, we do a lot of work for other units. Recently, for example, we had to revise a plan for an ammunition depot, which involved checking the distances between storage bunkers, the siting of blast walls, and a lot of other things to do with safety. We also had to make sure that the original plan was correct, and add on any new buildings which had been erected.

When we are revising a map, we have to take out the original with us. We make a note of anything marked on the map that is no longer on the ground – a hedge, say, that has been grubbed out – and of anything new. Then, back in the office, we copy out our plotting on to two sheets of transparent overlay. On the first, we ink out in red everything that has disappeared and, on the second, we ink in in black everything that is to be added.

Another job to be done in the office is writ-

Setting up the Aga 14. The corporal is removing the caps from the special prism which reflects the light beam.

A delicate instrument like a theodolite must be carefully maintained and cleaned regularly.

ing up a report of the survey you've just done. That has to be typed up and sent off to various people. All our information is also stored in a computer, which can do complicated things like working out areas and checking all our mathematical calculations. As a Tec 3 I'm not really required to know anything about computers – that's one of the things I'll learn on my Tec 2 course – but if there is no one around to handle it, I'm expected to open up the manual and learn as I go.

We normally work a five-day week here, but when we're out in the field we'll work non-stop. If the weather is fine we go out at first light and work right through until 8 or 9 o'clock at night, every day, until we get the job finished. When we're stuck back here in squadron H.Q. it can get a bit boring, because I'm either in the office or hanging round cleaning my kit and waiting for the next job to come in. At the moment, luckily, there's plenty to do!

One of the disadvantages of field survey is that you are limited in the places you can be posted to. There is a chance of going to Hong Kong, but that's only for a warrant officer. One of the best jobs of all is with a unit that moves around the world tracking satellites, but again that is only for staff sergeants and above.

It's difficult to tell how far I will be promoted. I don't think I'm a twenty-two year man – I've signed on for nine years, and I'll probably do an extra three to make it up to twelve, but after that I will seriously consider coming out of the Army. By that time I shall be in my mid-thirties, and finding a civilian job shouldn't be too difficult.

I believe I've learned a lot in the Army which will stand me in good stead outside. I did my survey course in seven months and started working at my trade straightaway, whereas if I'd stayed in civvy street it would

have taken me about five years to qualify, and I would probably have been a tea-boy for a couple of years after that. My military survey qualification is also one that is recognized by civilian firms as being equal to a civilian one.

Bob reads a print-out from the computer.

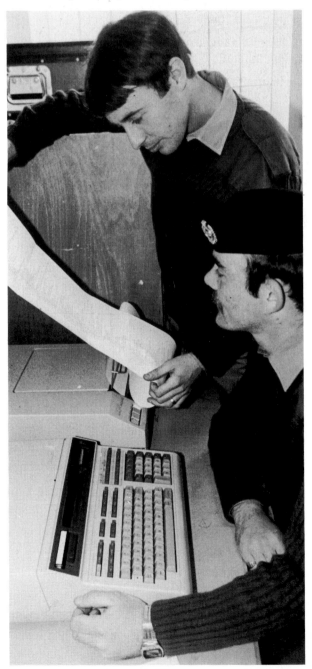

David Tucker
Bandsman

David Tucker is a lance sergeant and principal trombonist in the Scots Guards Band stationed in London. He is 28 years old and has been in the Army for twelve years.

The first army I ever joined was the Salvation Army! In Llanelli, in Wales, where I was born, my grandfather and my father both played in the band – and my grandfather became a Salvation Army colonel. So it was natural that I should be keen on playing a brass instrument, and I started with a trombone when I was only 7. It was a bit big for a young lad to handle, but my father helped me and gave me regular lessons. I used to go on Salvation Army camps where a lot of music teaching went on. I've never had to pay for a lesson in my life.

I left school at 15, and didn't really have much idea about what I wanted to do, except play my trombone. But you can't make a living out of that in South Wales. I started training as a carpet fitter in a local shop, but I never enjoyed it much because I didn't have any time for my music. So at 16 I left and signed up to join the Army, where I could actually get paid for doing what I liked doing, and see a bit of the world as well.

For the first few weeks, of course, I had no time even to touch my trombone. I joined the Royal Welch Fusiliers, who were my local regiment, and went straight to Crickhowell for my basic military training. Everyone who joins the Army has to go through this, even a bandsman like me who is never going to fight anyway. They teach you to march and salute and fire a gun, and make sure you can get a good spit-and-polish shine on your boots.

That lasted for four weeks, and then I went on to my band training. I already knew a bit about playing in a brass band, and about playing on the march, but here I had to learn everything again. There are four grades of army bandsman, and when you finish your first year of training, you have only reached Grade 4. If you are over 18 when you join up, you have to be better than Grade 4 already – and that means being able to sight-read.

Right after my training I was sent off with the regiment to Hong Kong. That was pretty lucky for a first posting, and I loved it out there. A year later I was back learning again, this time at the Royal Military School of Music, at Kneller Hall, near Twickenham. All bandsmen go there early in their careers, before the age of 23, to learn the more technical things about music – what they call music theory.

Our next tour of duty was eighteen months in Northern Ireland. The band didn't play at any ceremonies, of course. We were there to entertain the troops and their families, and to play concerts for the local children and at old folks' homes around Londonderry. At about this time I began to think of transferring to one of the Guards regiments. The standards of the Guards bands are very high indeed, and they will only take good and experienced musicians. Another advantage is that the Guards bands don't travel abroad with their regiment. They are stationed permanently in London, and only go abroad on special occasions.

However, my idea of transferring was knocked on the head for a while because the

Members of the band chat together before a performance.

David cleans his trombone after a day's practising.

Royal Welch Fusiliers sent me off for more training on Salisbury Plain. After that, I went for an audition to the Royal Scots Guards and was accepted – even though I am a Welshman! The only trouble was that when I transferred I lost all my rank. I was a lance corporal by then, but I had to go into the Guards as an ordinary musician.

The Guards regiments have a special set of ranks. We are always one rank higher than the ordinary regiments of the line. In the bands you start off as a musician, and then go straight up to corporal. The next rank is lance sergeant, followed by sergeant, colour sergeant and so on up to band sergeant-major, which is the highest non-commissioned rank.

I was made up to corporal after being fourteen months with the band. I've just taken the full sergeant's exams, and if I pass them, I may get promoted again, although I'll probably have to wait for the vacancies to come up. Some people have passed their exams all right, and have then had to wait for six years for a vacancy.

Life in the Guards band is a lot different from other regiments. For a start, we stay in London nearly all the time. We do our practising in the barracks in Victoria, and I live in married quarters up at Mill Hill. We play for most of the ceremonial occasions, like the Changing of the Guard and the Trooping the Colour, but we do get about a bit as well. Once we went out to Australia for three weeks, came back and went straight out to Kenya for three weeks, and then went on to Canada for a fortnight.

Usually we get abroad about three times a year. At the moment the battalion is stationed out in Hong Kong, and the band is going out there this autumn to entertain the troops and play at Government House – it's really a kind of holiday for us. If the battalion were much nearer – say in Germany – we would travel out there every year.

There are sixty-two people in the full band – flutes, oboes, clarinets, saxophones, a bassoon, horns, cornets, and trombones, euphoniums, basses and percussion. This is the band that does all the duty jobs, like Changing the Guard at Buckingham Palace and St. James's Palace. When it is our turn to do this, we march with a detachment of Guards from the barracks to the palaces, and play in the forecourt whilst the new Guard takes over from the old one that has been on duty for twenty-four hours. After the ceremone, we march back to barracks with the old Guard.

Our other big duties are the Trooping the Colour and the Festival of Remembrance. Standing at the Cenotaph in Whitehall with five bands on Remembrance Day is very moving – moments like that are really what you join up for in the first place. For these jobs we wear our ceremonial dress, the red coats, black trousers, white webbing and bearskin. When we are rehearsing, we wear what we

David and the band of the Royal Scots Guards rehearsing for the Trooping the Colour ceremony.

David in his full ceremonial outfit.

David and the band arrive with their instruments for a performance.

As well as his trombone, David also plays the violin.

call our 'blues', which are much plainer. Then, of course, we've got our ordinary working dress of khaki pullover, shirt and trousers for practising inside the barracks.

Being a Guards bandsman involves a lot more than playing on the big occasions. As one of the top military bands, we have to be able to produce a marching band, a concert band, a dance band, an orchestra and a fanfare team. The concert band gets about quite a lot, playing at places like the Albert Hall in London and the Fairfield Hall in Croydon, and doing one-night stands all over the country. Of course, the Scots Guards often go up to Scotland – we do plenty of concerts with Moira Anderson, for example.

The orchestra is made up of sixteen people, and its most important job is to play a programme of music inside Buckingham Palace during knighthood and medal ceremonies. It's also very popular for cabaret evenings in places like the Café Royal. You may find it odd to think of a Guards bandsman playing the violin, but you're only accepted into the band in the first place if you are proficient on two instruments – a brass one and a string one.

The Army gets paid privately for these outside jobs, and passes on about £12 to each bandsman who plays on them. If you do all the cabarets and concerts and so on, you can make an extra £900 a year, which comes in very handy. The main trouble is that only half of the people in the band are needed for them. We call these the 'Golden Thirty'. The Golden Thirty is made up, naturally enough, of the best musicians. I'm principal trombonist, so I go on all the paid jobs, but some of the others never do any of them at all. Competition inside the band for these jobs can be pretty fierce.

Actually, I have more work to do in the barracks than most people, because I'm also the assistant librarian. The actual librarian doesn't play in the band – he stays behind and sorts out the programmes. I help him by sorting out the 'march cards' every day. These are the little cards of march music which the musician fixes on to his instrument when he is marching along.

Because of this job (I don't get paid any extra for it, by the way) I have to get in earlier than the others in the morning, at 8.30. I pick out the right march cards for that day's work, and arrange them into little bundles which each man can store in his white card case, which hangs from his belt. We have a practice every weekday morning in the barracks, unless there is a Changing of the Guard to do. This lasts from about ten o'clock until half-past twelve, when most of them knock off for the day. I have to stay behind in the library until four o'clock sorting out the music.

It sounds like we have a short week, but

Before a performance, David hands out march cards to his fellow bandsmen.

David and his wife at home in their married quarters.

we've got to be prepared to sacrifice most of the weekend to play at concerts, tattoos and all the other events. And although we can go home at lunch-time, most of the afternoons are taken up with private practising and cleaning our uniforms and instruments. To be fair, the bandsmen do have a lot of time to earn extra money outside Army hours – especially if they're not one of the Golden Thirty. Most of them go teaching in schools, or playing in civilian bands and orchestras. They do all sorts of other jobs as well; there was even a craze a few months ago for working in betting shops!

Being the assistant librarian, I don't perhaps get as much chance as the others to earn extra money. But I get paid for all the private concerts so I don't really mind, and I still have plenty of time to spend with my wife in our married quarters. These are right on the edge of London, and a lot more quiet and peaceful than the unmarried quarters in the centre of town.

Appendices

Trades employed in the Army

There are over 150 trades and skills to be learned in the Army today, and they are divided into two categories. One is general (G) which requires a basic practical ability and a willingness to learn a job. The other is technical (T) which needs a high mental ability, to be able to cope with theoretical work and what is often a long period of training. The following is only a selection of the many trades.

The combat trades (including Infantry and Artillery)
Infantryman G
Parachutist G
Guardsman G
Sniper G
Gunner G
Combat Radioman G
Signaller G
Combat Engineer G
Bomb Disposal Engineer G
Assault Pioneer G
Radar Operator G
Driver (this includes various vehicles) G

Mechanical and scientific maintenance trades
Engineering Draughtsman T
Electrician G
Radio Technician T
Ammunition Technician T
Avionics Technician T
Electronics Technician T
Field Survey Technician T
Cartographic Technician T
Fitter G
Metalworker G
Aircraft Technician T
Gun Fitter G
Vehicle Mechanic G

Administration and transport trades
Clerk G
Storeman G
Air Despatcher G
Railwayman G
Seaman (Navigator) G
Crane Operator G
Recovery Mechanic G

Other specialist trades
Cook G
Bricklayer G
Carpenter G
Butcher G
Tailor G
Dog Trainer G
Bandsman G
Photographer G
State Registered Nurse T
Medical Assistant G

There are many more trades than those listed here. For a full list, see the Army booklet *Your Life in the Army*, available from your local Army Careers Information Office.

Sources of further information
If you are interested in finding out more about the Army, ask your careers teacher at school to put you in touch with the Schools Army Liaison Officer for your area. Otherwise, you are sure to find that there is an Army Careers Information Office near you. The address is in the phone book under 'Army'.
Some useful books are:
Joining the Army by Peter Douglas (Wayland)
A Day With a Soldier by Chris Fairclough (Wayland)
Soldiers in Battle by Kenneth Allen (Odhams)
Soldiering On by Dennis Barker (Deutsch)

Acknowledgements
The author and photographer would like to thank the many people in the Ministry of Defence and the Army without whose help this book could not have been written – especially John Turner, Jock Bennett, Derrick Knight and the twelve soldiers whose pictures and words appear in these pages.

Index